# Contents

Any words appearing in the text in bold, **like this**, are explained in the Glossary.

# A man 'for all time'

Around the year 1600, several theatres stood on the south bank of the River Thames in London. One of them, the Globe, allegedly had a Latin motto which in English means: 'All the world's a stage.' It was here that many plays by William Shakespeare, England's most famous playwright, were first performed. Today the whole world could be called a stage for the continuing presentation of the master playwright's works, whether on film, on TV or in the theatre.

Shakespeare – who was a wonderful poet as well as a dramatist – died almost four centuries ago but he still exerts an enormous cultural influence. A dozen of his plays deal with the history of England, especially in medieval times. Generations of people have relied, sometimes rightly but sometimes wrongly, on these stirring works for factual information on England's past. Shakespeare also continues to affect the way we speak as well as the way we think. Anyone who uses a phrase like 'the milk of human kindness', 'O brave new world', 'the winter of our discontent' or even 'my horse, my horse, my kingdom for a horse' is quoting, possibly without knowing it, from Shakespeare.

The British actor Joseph Fiennes played England's greatest writer in the hugely successful 1998 film *Shakespeare in Love*. It is unlikely that even in his younger, slimmer days, Shakespeare looked like this!

# William Shakespeare

## HAYDN MIDDLETON

**www.heinemann.co.uk/library**
Visit our website to find out more information about **Heinemann Library** books.

To order:
☎ Phone 44 (0) 1865 888066
🖹 Send a fax to 44 (0) 1865 314091
🖳 Visit the Heinemann Bookshop at www.heinemann.co.uk/library to browse our catalogue and order online.

First published in Great Britain by Heinemann Library, Halley Court, Jordan Hill, Oxford OX2 8EJ, a division of Reed Educational and Professional Publishing Ltd. Heinemann is a registered trademark of Reed Educational and Professional Publishing Ltd.

OXFORD MELBOURNE AUCKLAND JOHANNESBURG BLANTYRE GABORONE IBADAN PORTSMOUTH NH (USA) CHICAGO

© Reed Educational and Professional Publishing Ltd 2002.
First published in paperback 2003.
The moral right of the proprietor has been asserted.

Designed by Tinstar Design (www.tinstar.co.uk)
Originated by Ambassador Litho Ltd
Printed and bound by South China Printing Company Ltd in Hong Kong/China

ISBN 0 431 13995 4   (hardback)        ISBN 0 431 14002 2   (paperback)
06 05 04 03 02                         07 06 05 04 03
10 9 8 7 6 5 4 3 2 1                   10 9 8 7 6 5 4 3 2 1

**British Library Cataloguing in Publication Data**
Middleton, Haydn
      William Shakespeare. – (Creative Lives)
      1. Shakespeare, William, 1564–1616
      2. Dramatists, English – Early modern, 1500–1700 – Biography – Juvenile literature
      I.Title
      822.3'3

**Acknowledgements**
The Publishers would like to thank the following for permission to reproduce photographs:
Berkley Castle, Gloucestershire: p24; Bodleian Library: pp11, 25; Bridgeman Art Library: pp8, 16, 20, 35, 37, 40, 41, 55 (top); British Library: pp18, 22, 39, 46; Collections: Emma Wood, p5, Julian Nieman, p36; Hulton Archive: pp12, 13 (top), 19, 47; Kobal Collection: pp4, 30, 31 (top); Performing Arts Library: pp45, 52; Photostage: Donald Cooper, p55 (bottom); Public Record Office: pp14, 38, 50; Robert Harding Picture Library: Nigel Francis, p7; Ronald Grant Archive: pp28, 31 (bottom); Shakespeare Birthplace Trust: p42; Shakespeare Centre Library: pp9 (top and bottom), 13 (bottom), 27, 33, 34, 48.

Cover photograph reproduced with permission of Hulton Getty.

Our thanks to Stanley Wells for his assistance in the preparation of this book.

Every effort has been made to contact copyright holders of any material reproduced in this book. Any omissions will be rectified in subsequent printings if notice is given to the Publishers.

Since 1795 this house in Shottery, a mile west of Stratford-upon-Avon, has been called 'Anne Hathaway's Cottage'. Anne was the woman who in 1582 became William Shakespeare's wife. He was 18, she was 26. We have clear documentary proof of the marriage, as well as of other important moments in Shakespeare's life, but little 'everyday' information about him has survived.

His vocabulary was vast. Made up of over 21,000 words, including many he **coined** himself, it is probably the richest in English literature. The unique way in which he wove them together has established him as one of the best-known Englishmen of all time – maybe *the* best-known.

## Digging the dust

After his death in 1616, William Shakespeare was buried in Holy Trinity Church, Stratford-upon-Avon – the town where he was born in 1564. This verse was carved onto his gravestone:

*'GOOD FRIEND FOR JESUS SAKE FORBEARE*
*TO DIGG THE DUST ENCLOASED HERE.*
*BLESTE BE THE MAN THAT SPARES THES STONES*
*AND CURST BE HE THAT MOVES MY BONES.'*

('Good friend, for Jesu's sake **forbear**/To dig the dust enclosed here./Blessed be the man who spares these stones/And cursed be he that moves my bones.')

Many historians and biographers have tried to 'move the bones' of Shakespeare. They have tried to put flesh on them once more, and bring the literary genius back to life. Yet this has never been an easy task.

Some records relating to Shakespeare's life have survived – from his baptism to his burial, with certain other legal documents in between. And some of the buildings where he once spent time are still standing. There are also some references to him in the writings of his **contemporaries**. Yet we have little evidence about his character – what kind of son he was, what kind of husband and father, what kind of friend, what kind of 17th-century celebrity. To give us a sense of Shakespeare the man, later writers have had to use all their ingenuity, by reading between the lines of the dry legal documents, by looking for clues in the lines of his own plays and poems, and by making guesses based on the available information.

For all that, he remains elusive. We cannot be sure that the two existing contemporary images of him show a true likeness. We cannot even say for certain exactly how many plays he wrote. And so, because not even the most inspired scholar can ever really 'know' Shakespeare, people have often felt free to **romanticize** his life and personality. After his death, his friend and rival Ben Jonson said, 'He was not of an age, but for all time!' To many, he can seem as timeless as some of the masterpieces he wrote – like *Romeo and Juliet*, *The Merchant of Venice*, *A Midsummer Night's Dream*, *King Lear*, *Macbeth*

### 'Read him'

John Heminges and Henry Condell gathered together Shakespeare's plays for publication in 1623. They addressed these introductory words 'To the great Variety of Readers': 'His mind and hand went together, and what he thought, he uttered with that easiness that we have scarce received from him a blot in his papers. But it is not our **province**, who only gather his works and give them to you, to praise him. It is yours that read him. And there we hope, to your **divers** capacities, you will find enough, both to draw, and to hold you: for his **wit** can no more lie hid, than it could be lost. Read him, therefore; and again, and again.'

The Royal Shakespeare Theatre in Stratford, Shakespeare's birthplace in Warwickshire. This is one of the theatres that is home to the Royal Shakespeare Company, which also takes productions on tour around the UK and as far afield as the USA, Australia and India.

and *Othello*. But Shakespeare belonged very much to his own time too, living as a man among men and a working as a writer among writers. Not only did his genius lie in producing poetry and plays that still thrill us, but also in providing first-class entertainment for the audiences of **Tudor** and **Stuart** England.

### Did he really write the plays?

Shakespeare is a shadowy figure, and it is almost certain that he never went to university or travelled widely abroad. For these reasons some **critics** believe he could not have had the education or experience to produce such wonderful work. Some still claim that the plays must have been written by someone else entirely – maybe Shakespeare's fellow-playwright Christopher Marlowe, or the brilliant Francis Bacon, or even Queen Elizabeth I! But Shakespeare would have had a sound education at school in Stratford. And throughout his life he could have *read* about other lands even if he did not visit them. So there is little reason to suppose that he did not write the plays.

# 'Disturbers of the whole world'

In April 1564, a baby boy was born to John and Mary Shakespeare in Stratford-upon-Avon. This little market town lay in the heart of England, about a hundred miles north of the capital city, London. That was where the recently crowned Queen Elizabeth I held her court. Although London was only two to three days' ride away, few of Stratford's residents would ever have visited it. Throughout their lives, most **Tudor** people seldom ventured far from the places where they were born. The Queen's government discouraged all travel unless it was absolutely necessary. And the unemployed were punished if, in times of financial hardship, they took to the roads in search of work.

The baby born to the Shakespeares was registered after his baptism as 'Gulielmus', which was Latin for William. He was to be the eldest of their six surviving children, but two daughters had already died before he was born. Shakespeare himself could very easily have lived an equally short life. For in the summer of 1564 a wave of the plague struck the town and killed more than two hundred of its inhabitants.

*The Triumph of Death* by Dutch artist Pieter Brueghel shows the devastation that could be caused by the plague – alongside many other hazards of mid-16th-century life. It was painted in the 1560s, the decade of Shakespeare's birth.

This is Shakespeare's birthplace on Henley Street, Stratford – nowadays a hugely successful tourist attraction. In the parish register (bottom), his baptism was recorded on 26 April 1564. Since babies were baptized very soon after being born, it is possible that the actual date of his birth was 23 April – the feast day of Saint George, England's patron saint. We know for sure that he *died* on 23 April, 52 years later, in 1616.

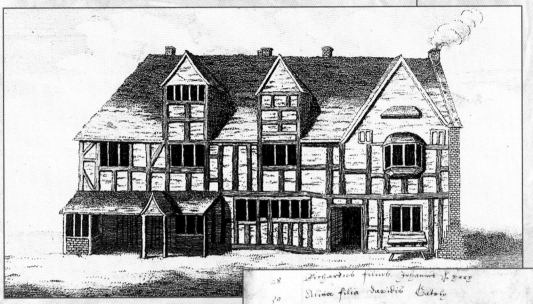

Although there were eventually eight of them, the Shakespeares lived in relative luxury by 16th-century standards. Shakespeare's father – a glover and **curer** of soft skins for gloves – made a good enough living to provide his family with a fine half-timbered house that still stands today. He became an important figure in the local community, reaching the position of **Bailiff** and owning several houses. One of his duties was to taste the beer brewed in Stratford to make sure its quality was maintained. He had married Mary, whose maiden name was Arden, between 1556 and 1558 and he lived until 1601. During his later years his fortunes mysteriously declined (see page14).

9

## The world of young William

In what kind of a world did the boy Shakespeare grow up? It is tempting to see it just as a quainter, slower version of our own world, with far fewer people in it. In fact there were some much more profound differences.

England and Scotland were then quite separate kingdoms, with their own royal families and their own kinds of national church. Religion was not a matter of purely personal preference. 'A state can never be in safety,' wrote Elizabeth I's chief minister William Cecil, 'where there is **toleration** of two religions. For there is no **enmity** so great as that over religion. And they that differ in their service of God, can never agree in the service of their country.'

This was a very common 16th-century view. In many parts of mainland Europe **Protestant** and **Catholic** forces were fighting bitter, savagely destructive wars against each other. Farther to the east, the mighty military empire of the Muslim Turks was threatening to conquer the entire Christian continent. Meanwhile ambitious European seamen were sailing out to make lasting contact with the 'New World' of the Americas and the mythically wealthy empires of the **Orient**.

Protestant England was a small kingdom in this rapidly expanding world. Unlike Catholic Spain and France it was not rich, nor did Elizabeth's government even have a regular **standing army** to call on in times of emergency. But as some Europeans began to identify themselves more strongly with their homelands, a number of Elizabeth's patriotic subjects proudly proclaimed that *their* country had special, magical, even holy qualities. Shakespeare was going to become one of them. A character in his historical play *Richard II* tenderly describes England as 'This precious stone set in the silver sea'.

Foreign observers did not always share this opinion. To many of them, England was an uncultured land full of unfriendly people, with a forbidding climate to match. The pirate raids of English seamen like Francis Drake on other countries' shipping further tarnished the name of England abroad. 'The English have become **odious** to all nations,'

### England as Faery land

Saint George, England's patron saint, slays the dragon in this engraving from *The Faerie Queen*, a verse epic by the great Elizabethan poet, Edmund Spenser (1552–99). Spenser wrote that Gloriana, the central figure of his great poem, was based on 'the most excellent and glorious person of our **sovereign**

the Queen, and her kingdom in Faery land.' (Other figures in his poem came from British mythology – like King Lear, whom Shakespeare himself later turned into the hero of a play.) Queen Elizabeth I ably ruled over Protestant England for more than 40 years until 1603. 'I know I have the body of a weak and feeble woman,' she declared in 1588, 'but I have the heart and stomach of a king, and a king of England too.'

wrote a Venetian ambassador in 1603. 'They are the disturbers of the whole world.' But it was from this 'odious' nation that the uniquely gifted poet and playwright William Shakespeare was to arise and take his place on the world's stage.

# Family man

In **Tudor** England, no child *had* to go to school. In many places there were no schools to go to; and besides, poorer parents often needed to set their children to practical work as soon as they were physically able. But in 1561, John Shakespeare was elected a Stratford **burgess**. One of his perks was that he could send his sons, free of charge, to the town's grammar school. (In those days daughters were usually educated at home – in subjects that were domestically useful rather than strictly intellectual.) We know that despite his later brilliance, John's son William never attended university. But he must have spent some years at the King's New School, Stratford, after the age of six.

## Tudor schooling

Educational methods varied from school to school in later Tudor times. It was, however, generally believed that sin lurked in all children – and had to be beaten out of them if they were to grow into responsible adults. Even the relatively blameless could suffer: teachers at Westminster School picked monitors from among the most serious schoolboys to watch over the rest and stop 'anything dirty' from being done. Monitors who did not do their duty properly could

Here Elizabeth I hunts near Kenilworth Castle, home of her **suitor** the Earl of Leicester. For three weeks in 1575 the Earl lavishly entertained the Queen there – laying on plays, fireworks and other spectacles. The 11-year-old Shakespeare, who lived close by, may have been among the crowds with his father. Five years later, he may also have watched the cycle of **mystery plays** that was performed in nearby Coventry. If so, it may have whetted his appetite for the dramatic life.

be flogged hard themselves. With pupils also having to attend lessons for up to ten hours a day, six days a week, it is little wonder that school holidays were sometimes called 'remedies'!

All schoolwork was based on the study of Latin. This was not then a dead, ancient language; it was also still widely used by statesmen, scholars and officials throughout western Europe. (As we have seen on page 8, Shakespeare's own baptism was registered in Latin.) Schoolboys read and translated comedies by the Roman dramatists Terence and Plautus as well as the poetry of Ovid. Books were in short supply, therefore long passages had to be learned by heart. Some of the classwork was also acted out in short scenes and dialogues. All this might have had a particular value for a budding actor and playwright.

A schoolroom scene from the 16th century shows a time when corporal punishment was not forbidden.

This was Shakespeare's schoolroom, only a quarter of a mile from his home in Henley Street, Stratford.

In *As You Like It*, Shakespeare described:
'... the whining schoolboy, with his satchel,
And shining morning face, creeping like snail
Unwillingly to school.'

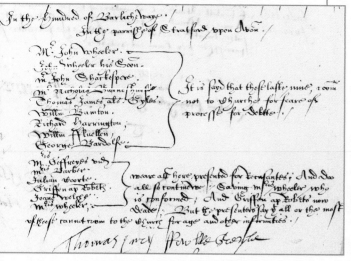

Was he writing from experience? In his comedy *The Merry Wives of Windsor*, he wrote a funny scene featuring a boy called William and a Welsh schoolmaster. Was this too based on his own youth? One of the masters at the King's New School, Thomas Jenkins, happens to have been a Welshman.

## Hard times in Henley Street

It is possible that Shakespeare did not complete his course of study at school. His family had grown to a considerable size: his brother Gilbert was born in 1566, his sister Joan in 1569, Anne in 1571, Richard in 1574 and lastly Edmund in 1580. Meanwhile his father's career had taken a turn for the worse. In 1568, he had become **Bailiff**, a kind of mayor of Stratford. And around 1575 he applied for a **coat of arms**, which was a sure sign of worldly success. Yet after that date he fell into debt, bought no more land and ceased to work for the town council. He may simply have fallen foul of an **economic recession** which hit all England in later Tudor times. Some scholars have also suggested that he fell from favour because he was a sympathizer with the **Catholics**, or even a Catholic himself. In which case, was his son one too?

Whatever the family's religion, the younger Shakespeare probably assisted the elder in preparing skins for glove-making. Until 1592, nothing is known about how he earned his living. He may have served for a while as a teacher of 'petties' or pre-grammar school children. He may have worked as a lawyer's clerk in the town, since legal terms often appear in the plays he wrote later. In the absence of reliable records, we can only speculate. But three hard facts *do* survive from these years. For each we have the documents to prove them. First,

Shakespeare got married, then he had a daughter, then he had twins. If he had had any ambitions to go to university or officially learn a trade, this was the end of them. For both **undergraduates** and apprentices had to be **bachelors**.

## 'Hate away' to Hathaway?

Shakespeare was eighteen when he married Anne Hathaway. Anne, the orphaned daughter of a farmer, was around eight years older. She must have been pregnant at the time of the marriage, since she gave birth to their first child, Susanna, within six months. The baby was baptised on 26 May 1583. Then on 2 February 1585 a twin girl and boy, Judith and Hamnet, were baptized. They all probably lived with the rest of Shakespeare's family in Henley Street. In those times of hardship, it must have been a struggle to keep all the mouths fed.

Did Shakespeare marry Anne for love? She certainly brought little wealth with her. Did they stay in love, although sometimes living apart, through more than 33 years of marriage? Most experts believe not. Yet the man who created some of the greatest love poetry of all time, may have written his first verse about her. In a poem now known simply as **Sonnet** 145, he wrote the lines below. Could the last-but-one line be a pun on the name 'Hathaway' or 'Hattaway', which was an alternative way of spelling his wife's name?

'Those lips that love's own hand did make
Breathed forth the sound that said "I hate",
To me, that **languished** for her sake;
But when she saw my woeful state,
Straight in her heart did mercy come,
**Chiding** that tongue that, ever sweet,
Was used in giving gentle doom,
And taught it thus anew to greet:
"I hate" she altered with an end
That followed it as gentle day
Doth follow night, who like a fiend
From heaven to hell is flown away.
    "I hate" from "hate" away she threw,
    And saved my life, saying "not you".'

# Theatreland

In 1592, the bookstalls in St Paul's Churchyard, London, were selling a new publication by Robert Greene, a Cambridge University graduate, poet, prose-writer and playwright. This autobiographical work, entitled *Greene's Groatsworth of* **Wit** (a groat was a small coin), featured the following angry passage. Difficult to understand today, it is addressed to three 'fellow scholars about this city', one of whom was the celebrated Christopher Marlowe:

'… there is an upstart Crow, beautified with our feathers, that with his *tiger's heart wrapped in a player's hide* supposes he is as well able to bombast out a blank verse as the best of you; and, being an absolute *Johannes Factotum*, is in his own conceit the only Shake-scene in a country…'

The first italic phrase is drawn from one of William Shakespeare's earliest plays, *Henry VI Part 3*, and the word 'Shake-scene' is a play on the name of its author. This is, in fact, an attack on a new talent in town – an 'upstart' with no university education (unlike other famous playwrights) and a '*Johannes Factotum*' (Jack of all trades) who possibly adapted the plays of others as well as writing his own. This is the first written evidence that Shakespeare of Stratford-upon-Avon had become well-known in London, as a 'player' (actor) and writer. Later documents show that by the 1590s he was living and working in the city.

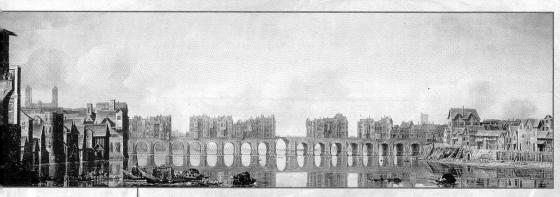

London, with a population of around 200,000 people, covered a much smaller area in the 1590s than it does today. Grand buildings like the Tower, the Royal Exchange and the old St Paul's Cathedral dwarfed the cramped slums of the poor as well as the homes of the fabulously rich. Running past the warrens of streets and alleys, the River Thames – spanned by just one bridge – was by far the busiest highway in the city.

## A Queen's Man?

Why had he made the long journey to the capital? When did he make it? And why did he not bring the rest of his family, who continued to live in Stratford? The answer to all three questions is that we do not know. The sources are silent about the period between the birth of his twins Judith and Hamnet in 1585 and Greene's back-handed tribute to him in 1592. But at some time during these seven 'lost years' Shakespeare stepped into the world of the theatre and then he never left it.

It is possible that he first left his home town by joining a touring company of actors. **Troupes** based in London often appeared in Stratford to put on shows in the Gild Hall, and maybe also in the inn-yards of Bridge Street. In 1583–4, companies under the **patronage** of the earls of Oxford, Essex and Worcester performed in Stratford. In the year after December 1586 no fewer than five passed through the town. One of them, the Queen's Men, may have arrived in Stratford short of one actor – in that year William Knell was killed in a duel. Did the 23-year-old Shakespeare join up to replace him?

### Foreign fans of the London theatres

In 1598, Paul Hentzner, a German visitor, described 'some Theatres (all built of wood), where English actors represent almost every day **tragedies** and **comedies** to very numerous audiences; these are concluded with excellent music, variety of dances, and the excessive applause of those that are present.' The Swiss Thomas Platter noted in 1599: 'Every day around two o'clock in the afternoon in the city of London two and sometimes even three plays are performed at different places, in order to make people merry… The places are built in such a way that they act on a raised scaffold, and everyone can well see everything. However, there are separate galleries and places, where one sits more pleasantly and better, therefore also pays more. For he who remains standing below pays only one English penny, but if he wants to sit… he gives another penny.'

Once settled in London, he did not send for his family – maybe because the teeming, unhygienic city was not an ideal place to raise children. But he kept returning to Stratford. As his fame and wealth increased he bought more property there too, before going back to spend his final years in the small Warwickshire town. London seems seldom to have inspired his creative imagination, for he wrote about it less than fellow playwrights like Ben Jonson or Thomas Dekker. In the words of Wendy Greenhill: 'His plays inhabit countries of the mind – imagined France or Italy, or more often what seems like rural Warwickshire recreated in a loving dream.'

The first purpose-built, permanent theatre probably dated from 1567. This was the Red Lion in Whitechapel, but it lasted for only a few months. Later theatres like the Rose and the Swan were clustered just south of the river. Shakespeare may have known them – acting in some, writing or adapting plays in others. However big a name the 'upstart Crow' was making for himself, he was by no means London

THE

SPANISH TRAGE-
die, Containing the lamentable
end of *Don Horatio*, and *Bel-imperia*:
with the pittifull death of
olde *Hieronimo*.

Newly corrected and amended of such grosse faults as
passed in the first impression.

AT LONDON
Printed by *Edward Allde*, for
Edward White.

This is an early copy of *The Spanish Tragedy*, which was an enormously popular and bloodthirsty play by Thomas Kyd (1558–94) from around the year 1586. Playwrights had little control over their finished work. They sold plays to their theatrical companies, whose actors often tried to stop them from being printed. For once a 'playbook' appeared on the stalls, anyone could buy it and have it produced.

theatreland's only celebrity. Thomas Kyd, Christopher Marlowe, Thomas Nashe and, a little later, Ben Jonson were all fine and popular writers. More than two hundred plays by Shakespeare's fellow dramatists have survived from the decades on either side of the year 1600 – a golden age in the history of English theatre.

In 1596, a Dutch visitor to London made this drawing of the Swan theatre. Note the absence of scenery and the open roof, as in a modern football stadium. 'Theatres are the meeting places for thieves, horse stealers and other idle and dangerous persons,' claimed the Lord Mayor of London in 1597. But people from all walks of life watched plays – and gave noisy verdicts on them, whether positive or negative.

# Poet and sharer

When Robert Greene made his attack on Shakespeare in 1592, he called him a '*Johannes Factotum*', a Jack of all trades. He meant it as a term of abuse. (A Jack of all trades is supposed to be a master of none.) But in that year – and in the two after it – Shakespeare's versatility stood him in very good stead. For during that period, thanks to a severe outbreak of plague, the theatres had to close and Shakespeare turned to writing non-dramatic poetry to earn his living. In doing so, he proved that a genius can be a master of more than one 'trade'.

## Taking advantage of idle hours

'The cause of plagues is sin, if you look to it well; and the cause of sins are plays: therefore the cause of plagues are plays.' So claimed a preacher at St Paul's Cross before the plague outbreak of 1592–4. More and more **Puritan**-minded people saw theatres as **dens of iniquity**. Meanwhile the authorities correctly believed that any large crowd was 'perilous for **contagion**'. So at least until the epidemic passed, public plays were banned. Shakespeare, like other playwrights, may well have wondered if the theatres would ever open again.

This portrait shows Shakespeare's **patron**, Henry Wriothesley, 3rd Earl of Southampton. He was just 19 years old when Shakespeare dedicated *Venus and Adonis* to him, and fell from the Queen's favour in 1601 when he backed the Earl of Essex in an attempted **coup**. Here he is shown imprisoned in the Tower of London, accompanied by a black-and-white cat. According to legend, it joined him by climbing down a chimney.

All printed books were recorded on a list called the Stationers' Register. On 18 April 1593, the printer Richard Field, also a Stratford man, entered a new title. It was the long, erotic and often comic poem *Venus and Adonis* by William Shakespeare. Then on 9 May 1594, a different printer, John Harrison, registered another Shakespeare poem, *The Rape of Lucrece*. At 1855 lines, it was the length of a short play – and today it can seem even longer, since it is, as one modern scholar has called it, 'perhaps the only joke-free zone in the whole of Shakespeare's works'!

Both poems were inspired by works by the ancient Roman writer Ovid. Shakespeare completely rewrote them in his wonderfully inimitable style – and thanks to their sales he not only began to establish a reputation as a fine writer, but also made some money. He improved this wealth considerably by winning the patronage of Henry Wriothesley (see picture). Shakespeare dedicated both poems to the young Earl of Southampton, using the standard **fawning** language of the time. 'Only,' he wrote, 'if your honour seem but pleased, I account myself highly praised; and vow to take advantage of all idle hours, till I have honoured you with some graver labour.' In return for such flattery, a creative artist could secure the backing of an influential friend. This could be very useful in such unpredictable times.

### The 'graver labour'

The 'graver labour' that Shakespeare promised his patron the Earl of Southampton, in his dedication of *Venus and Adonis*, turned out to be *The Rape of Lucrece*. 'The love I dedicate to your Lordship is without end,' wrote the poet in the opening **epistle**. Here are some lines from late in the poem, describing blood pouring from the heroine's stabbed body:

'And bubbling from her breast, it doth divide
In two slow rivers, that the crimson blood
Circles her body in on every side,
Who like a late-sack'd island vastly stood
Bare and unpeopled in this fearful flood.
        Some of her blood still pure and red remain'd,
        And some look'd black, and that false Tarquin stain'd.'

Here we see the title page of Shakespeare's first publication, the poem *Venus and Adonis* from 1594. The author's name, not yet a selling point, does not appear upon it. But the volume was very successful, with multitudes buying and enjoying it. By 1640, it had already gone through sixteen **editions**. No other work by Shakespeare had as many printings during this period.

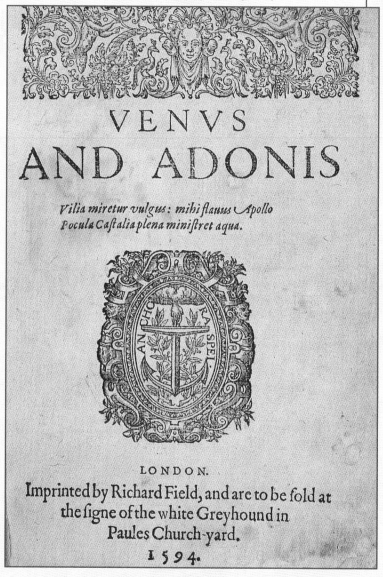

## Lord Chamberlain's Man

The London theatres did re-open after the plague passed, and Shakespeare soon went back to dramatic work. We know this because a document exists from early in 1595. This source lists payments that were made by the Queen for two theatrical performances at her royal palace in Greenwich in late 1594.

The players being paid belonged to a **troupe** known as the Lord Chamberlain's Men. We have the names of three of its leading members who received payment in 1595: William Kempe, Richard Burbage and the now 30-year-old William Shakespeare. We do not know what plays were put on for the Queen. Probably they were by Shakespeare himself. But although there are legends telling of her great love for his work, there is no documentary proof that 'Gloriana' looked on his plays with special favour.

The Lord Chamberlain's Men, unlike some other companies, was an established troupe of actors which for many years enjoyed great success on London's stages. The more successful the company was, the more Shakespeare benefited. For he not only wrote and acted in its plays, he also invested some of his funds in it, in return for a share of the profits it made. For this reason he was known as a 'sharer' – what we might call a shareholder. The company's actors did not perform *only* plays written by Shakespeare, but he was employed to write only for them. Thus he was London's first 'playwright in residence'; the troupe's own term for him was their 'ordinary poet'.

The sums of money that he made from his dramatic work, whether in poetry or prose, were far from ordinary. Scholars disagree on exactly how much he earned annually after becoming a 'hit' writer. But it seems likely that while writing on average two theatrical pieces annually, he made about £200 per year. That was ten times the salary of the well-paid Stratford schoolmaster – a handsome reward for an 'upstart' playwright from the **provinces** with no university education and little family wealth.

On page 48 you can find out how he invested some of his riches back in his home town of Stratford. Although he must often have travelled back to see his family, his base continued to be in the capital. In 1597, he was living in St Helen's **parish** in the City of London. By 1600, he had moved to the south bank of the Thames – the 'theatreland' where many playhouses stood. We know his whereabouts at these times since he was listed then for failing to pay his taxes.

## The Lord Chamberlain

This portrait portrays Lord Chamberlain Hunsdon, in 1591. Shakespeare worked exclusively for his theatrical company from 1594. The first cousin of Queen Elizabeth I, Hunsdon's full name and title were Henry Carey, 1st Baron Hunsdon, and he lived from 1526 until 1596. He became Lord Chamberlain in 1585, and when the Spanish Armada tried to land in 1588 he commanded the English troops at Tilbury. He was said to be 'unpolished' and excitable, with an awesome capacity for swearing. Soon after his death, his son Sir George Carey was appointed Lord Chamberlain and he continued keenly to protect and promote the interests of the Lord Chamberlain's Men.

## Keeping the customers satisfied

Two other leading Lord Chamberlain's Men were named in the document of 1595. One was Richard Burbage, the other was Will Kempe. In late **Tudor** London, both these actors were at least as famous as Shakespeare himself. Burbage, coming from a well-known theatrical family, was the great tragic hero of the age. Kempe excelled in comic roles.

So popular were they that their fellow sharer Shakespeare tailored parts in his plays to suit their special talents. Throughout history, it has not been unusual for writers or composers to create works with particular performers in mind. (The modern playwright Samuel Beckett wrote parts for the gifted actress Billie Whitelaw, while the composer Benjamin Britten wrote music for the supreme tenor voice of the singer Peter Pears.)

## Tailor-made parts

The comic actor and dancer Will Kempe is shown here performing a morris dance all the way from London to Norwich. We know that he played Peter in Shakespeare's *Romeo and Juliet* and Dogberry in his *Much Ado About Nothing*. It is also likely that he first played Bottom in *A Midsummer Night's Dream*, a comic role well-suited to his extrovert character. Richard Burbage played the lead in demanding Shakespearean tragedies such as *Hamlet*, *Othello* and *King Lear*. His father James, originally a carpenter, built London's first permanent playhouse, the Theatre, which was where the Lord Chamberlain's Men performed.

Kemps nine daies vvonder.

Performed in a daunce from
London to Norwich.

Containing the pleasure, paines and kinde entertainment
of *William Kemp* betweene *London* and that Citty
in his late Morrice.

Wherein is somewhat set downe worth note; to reprooue
the slaunders spred of him: many things merry,
nothing hurtfull.

*Written by himselfe to satisfie his friends.*

LONDON
Printed by *E. A.* for *Nicholas Ling*, and are to be
folde at his shop at the west doore of Saint
Paules Church. 1600.

Tudor and **Stuart** audiences flocked to see Shakespeare's plays not just to be impressed by the playwright's way with words, or his grasp of history, or his understanding of human nature. They also came to be entertained by their favourite players. Shakespeare was lucky to have such brilliant actors as Burbage and Kempe to deliver his lines. But they, too, were lucky to perform in plays written by a literary genius who knew how to keep all the customers satisfied – whether they happened to be noblemen or apprentice boys.

# The fantastic 1590s

In Shakespeare's time, not all playwrights saw their own works in print. Ben Jonson (1572–1637), a friend and rival of Shakespeare's, made sure that his own plays were printed and published during his lifetime so that he got the full credit for them. His works included *Volpone* (1605) and *The Alchemist* (1610), both of which are still staged today. In another play, *Every Man in His Humour*, we know that Shakespeare the actor was the leading 'principal comedian' at its original performance in 1598.

This piece of information comes from the **edition** of Jonson's works that was compiled in 1616 – the year of Shakespeare's death (see page 51). Seven years later two friends of Shakespeare's, John Heminges and Richard Condell, gathered up the texts of 36 of Shakespeare's plays and had them published in a 900-page book known as the First Folio. In a kind of introduction, some of Shakespeare's admirers wrote poems and letters about his genius. Jonson penned the poem in which he called him a man 'for all time' (see page 6).

## Comedies, histories and tragedies

The First Folio preserved almost all of Shakespeare's matchless work for posterity. Other sources might give the names of the plays that

### Prolific and unparalleled

Shakespeare became a huge success during the 1590s – a time when he had few rivals as a top London playwright. Robert Greene died in 1592, Christopher Marlowe in 1593 and Thomas Kyd in 1594, while Ben Jonson wrote his first successful comedy only in 1598. Shakespeare created at a steady rate, writing two or three plays each year; by the end of the century he had written around twenty. Almost always they were 'hits' with the public; Richard III's cry of 'A horse, a horse, my kingdom for a horse', in the play named after him, became an instant catchphrase. Some of Shakespeare's late Tudor plays are undisputed masterpieces. All contain passages of great beauty, and a profound understanding of acting and stagecraft.

## Shakespeare's likeness?

This is the **frontispiece** of the First Folio of Shakespeare's plays, published in 1623, seven years after he died. The portrait was engraved by Martin Droeshout, a 22-year-old member of a family of Flemish artists. Droeshout probably never saw Shakespeare alive, and worked from a line drawing made by someone older. Ben Jonson wrote about the image: 'Reader, look/Not on his picture, but his book'. That might suggest – according to the Shakespeare scholar Katherine Duncan-Jones – that it was not a good likeness. But it has been reproduced so often that many people now believe that Shakespeare looked just like this.

Mr. WILLIAM

# SHAKESPEARES

COMEDIES,
HISTORIES, &
TRAGEDIES.

Publifhed according to the True Originall Copies.

*LONDON*
Printed by Ifaac Iaggard, and Ed. Blount. 1623.

brought him fame and fortune in the 1590s, but in the First Folio we can read the actual plays. Scholars dispute the exact order in which they appeared. But we know for sure that each of the following well-known plays was written before the end of the century: *Romeo and Juliet*, *The Merchant of Venice*, *Julius Caesar*, *Henry V*, *Richard III* and *A Midsummer Night's Dream*. What sort of plays were they?

As you can see from the frontispiece to the First Folio, Heminges and Condell divided all the plays into 'Comedies, Histories, & Tragedies'. Scholars agree that much of Shakespeare's earlier work belonged in the category of 'Histories'. He wrote two cycles of four plays each, known as 'tetralogies', about kings of England during the previous 200 years. The first featured three plays about Henry VI (1422–61) and a fourth about Richard III (1483–85). The second, set further back

This scene comes from a film of Shakespeare's *Richard III*, released in 1995. The action has been transferred to a make-believe England of the 1930s. Richard (far left) has risen to power as a villainous abuser of power like Adolf Hitler in 1930s Germany. Henry Tudor – the grandfather of Elizabeth I, who ruled when Shakespeare wrote the play – finally kills the evil Richard to rescue the kingdom.

in the past, consisted of one play about Richard II (1377–99), two about Henry IV (1399–1413) and one about Henry V (1413–22). These were turbulent times for the English people. The first four kings either took or lost their thrones by force – while the fifth, Henry V, led the English in a momentous war against the French.

The struggle for power in England came to a head in the 15th-century 'Wars of the Roses', a lengthy series of civil wars that ended only after the **Tudor** monarchs fully established themselves.

## Shakespeare and history

Today, creative artists are often congratulated for producing work that is weird, original or out of the ordinary. In Shakespeare's time, playwrights normally presented characters and situations that were not alien, but accessible. This gives many of their plays a timeless, 'universal' quality. This universal appeal makes them seem as familiar and relevant now as when they were first performed. Indeed, they are often staged in modern dress, or set in periods long after Shakespeare himself lived.

Playwrights often took already familiar stories, then told them in new ways, adding provocative twists for greater effect. That was what the public was prepared to pay to see. For fictional plays like *Romeo and Juliet*, Shakespeare happily lifted his plots from existing sources, then re-arranged them in his own masterly way. Maybe more surprisingly, he also based the plots of his non-fictional plays on people and events from history – then sometimes re-arranged the facts and invented whole new episodes. This was either to make the plots more exciting for his audiences, or to put across a particular message to them – for example, about the nature of power and kingship. So in this sense, some of his history plays are not entirely historical.

One play in which Shakespeare took many liberties with historical truth was *Richard III*. Richard was the last king to reign before the Tudor **dynasty** came to power. Shakespeare portrayed him as a deformed, inhuman, child-murdering monster: 'that bottled spider, that foul, hunchback'd toad,' as the fictional Queen Elizabeth calls him in the play. The historical evidence for this is rather thin. But Shakespeare was keen to blacken the reputation of Richard in order to make his Tudor successors, who still ruled the country, appear far more appealing by comparison.

Shakespeare was subtly writing **propaganda** here in support of his country's rulers. In other plays too, he made it clear that rebellion against the rightly crowned monarch could lead only to disaster. We cannot be sure how seriously Shakespeare's audiences took these 'lessons' as part of their entertainment. But in such uncertain times, monarchs needed all the propagandist help they could get if they were to stay on their thrones. As Shakespeare himself pointed out in *Henry IV Part 2*: 'Uneasy lies the head that wears a crown.'

## Comedies and tragedies

The genres (another word for literary categories) of **comedy** and **tragedy** go back to ancient Greek times. The Greek writer Aristotle claimed that tragedy was superior to comedy because tragedies present people as better than the norm, while comedies present them as worse. Shakespeare's earlier tragedies were mainly set in the past (although they were not technically 'histories'). Often they involved an important man who underwent many trials before losing his life. The hero might be brought down by the workings of fate, or doomed by a fatal flaw in himself – like pride or jealousy.

This scene originates from the 1953 film of *Julius Caesar*, one of Shakespeare's early tragedies. Caesar (100 BC–44 BC) was a real Roman general and politician. He was assassinated by several fellow Romans who believed that power had gone to his head and was making him a danger to the state. In a sense, Caesar brought about his own downfall. 'The fault lies not in our stars,' Caesar says, 'but in ourselves.'

But Shakespeare was nothing if not versatile. During the 1590s he proved to be just as gifted at writing light, largely romantic comedies, often with plenty of scope for illusion and deception. Even so, a Shakespearean comedy was usually far more than a string of good jokes. *The Merchant of Venice*, for example, would have made audiences laugh a lot, yet it also explores the deeply serious matters of justice and the way that Christians and Jews relate to each other.

Although *Romeo and Juliet* starts with romance, it ends in tragedy. The young hero and heroine are destroyed by forces greater than themselves. Although they are deeply in love, their families, the Montagues and the Capulets, are involved in a bitter feud. Love and hate are irreconcilable and the lovers' tragic deaths follow.

'As Plautus and Seneca are accounted the best for comedy and tragedy among the **Latins**, so Shakespeare among the English is most excellent in both kinds for the stage.' So said Francis Meres, a student and keen theatre-goer, writing in 1598.

Shakespeare's original audiences may have heard echoes of the disastrous rivalry between the York and Lancaster families that erupted into the 15th-century 'Wars of the Roses'.

Claire Danes and Leonardo Di Caprio star in the 1996 film *William Shakespeare's Romeo and Juliet*. It was set not in Verona, Italy, but in Verona Beach, Florida.

A character in *Hamlet* – a marvellous tragic work written in about 1600 – made a list of all the possible types of play: 'tragedy, comedy, history, **pastoral**, pastoral-comical, historical-pastoral, tragical-historical, tragical-comical-historical-pastoral.' It is probably best to approach and enjoy each of Shakespeare's plays on its own terms, as a unique piece of art and entertainment.

This is a scene from *A Midsummer Night's Dream*, a wonderfully imaginative and sometimes disturbing play, full of transformations and magic, written around 1595. 'I have had a most rare vision,' says Bottom the weaver at one point. 'I have had a dream past the **wit** of man to say what dream it was.'

31

# Home from home

We cannot be sure how often Shakespeare travelled home to Stratford. He was a very busy man, and just the journey from London and back again would have taken up most of a week. Sometimes he may have found it easier to visit his parents, wife and children in Henley Street while he was making short tours of the **provinces** with the Lord Chamberlain's Men. We know of his presence in Stratford only if he had legal business there, which was then preserved in documents. But he must have made every effort to be with his family on or soon after 11 August 1596. For that was when the burial of his son Hamnet was recorded. The boy was just eleven and a half years old.

## The end of the line

In *Julius Caesar* Shakespeare wrote of an 'insupportable and touching loss.' Although we have no evidence of Shakespeare's own grief in 1596, the loss of his only son and heir must have been similarly affecting. The cause of Hamnet's early **demise** is unknown. His twin Judith lived on until the great age, in those days, of 70. But although both she and her sister Susanna married and had children, Hamnet's death doomed the male line of the Shakespeare family to extinction. In fact Susanna's daughter Elizabeth, who lived from 1608 until 1670, was Shakespeare's last direct relative.

Later in the sad year of 1596, the prosperous playwright may, however, have helped to bring honour to his family. Twenty years earlier, his father John had applied to be granted the official **status** of a 'gentleman'. This would have allowed him to display a **coat of arms** (see picture). Many Tudor families, especially in the middle ranks of society, were obsessed with their 'standing'. The grant of gentle status was a kind of proof that they were on their way up.

In the 1570s, John Shakespeare's application was turned down. But despite all his financial problems, he remained respected in Stratford and, possibly with the support of his famous son in 1596, his second application was successful. William too stood to gain from the grant. He now became the son of a gentleman. And when his father died in 1601 he became the head of a 'gentle' family.

## The Shakespeare family coat of arms

This was the coat of arms granted to Shakespeare's father in 1596. Such coats of arms were painted, embroidered, gilded or carved on a man's furniture, windows and even clothing. Featuring a falcon and a spear, this one was covered almost entirely with gold and silver (ordinary colours would have been cheaper to reproduce).

It carries the medieval French motto: *Non Sans Droict* ('Not Without Right'), meaning that John Shakespeare was well entitled to the arms. But it seems that neither he nor his descendants used the motto.

William may also have helped John to pay for this honour. A **patent** of gentility, plus all the expenses required to display the coat of arms, could have cost as much as £100. By comparison, the fine house into which the newly gentle Shakespeare family moved in 1597 may have cost 'sixty pounds in silver'. This dwelling, a 'pretty house of brick and timber', was called New Place. Built in the 15th century by Hugh Clopton, a locally born **mercer** and **benefactor** of the town, it was the second largest house in Stratford. Although in need of repair, New Place had no fewer than ten fireplaces – and there were probably more rooms than fireplaces. It stood in large gardens which later became famous for a mulberry tree and some flourishing vines. This was the home of a family that had made good in a **conspicuous** way.

At times, however, Shakespeare misused his wealth. A Stratford record from 1598 showed him hoarding ten **quarters** of corn and malt, for brewing. This was after a succession of bad harvests, and many of the poorer townspeople were starving. In a recent study of Shakespeare's life, Katherine Duncan-Jones pointed out that the great man showed little public spirit in other ways too. Unlike Hugh Clopton in Stratford or fellow celebrity actors like Edward Alleyn in Dulwich, Shakespeare seemed slow to use his riches for charitable ends. (Whereas Alleyn actively collected parish dues that provided **alms** for the poor, Shakespeare avoided paying his *own* dues!)

Instead he invested in land and more property, and may also have made loans to those in need. Then when he came to make his will, his 'tight-fistedness' seems to have extended to his own wife (see page 49). In Shakespeare's tragedy *Othello*, the villainous character Iago advises: 'Put money in thy purse.' Shakespeare himself appears to have taken that advice to heart, possibly because in his youth he had known what it was like to be without money.

## Crossing the river

Until late in his life, London remained Shakespeare's main base. From 1599 we believe he was living south of the river, in the **parish** of St Saviour's, Southwark. More intriguingly, his company's main theatre had crossed the river too – at dead of night. It happened like this...

This drawing of New Place was made by George Vertue in 1737. By then the house had come back into the possession of the Clopton family which originally built it. It was demolished in 1759. Only a well and a few foundation stones remain today. But an ancient mulberry tree – grown from one that Shakespeare himself supposedly planted – stands in the surviving 'Great Garden'.

This drawing of the Globe theatre was based on Claes Jan Visscher's view of London, 1616. When the Globe was built, James Burbage's sons could raise only 50 per cent of the cost. So five of the shareholders in the Lord Chamberlain's Men, including Shakespeare, put up 10 per cent each to make up the rest of the total. This gave the playwright a lucrative ten per cent share in the Globe enterprise.

The Globe

Until 1598, the Lord Chamberlain's Men performed at a playhouse in the north of London. Called the Theatre, it had been purpose-built by James Burbage, but it stood on land belonging to one Giles Allen. In 1598, a year after the death of Burbage, the lease on the playhouse expired, and Allen showed little interest in renewing it. In fact he made plans 'to pull down the same, and to convert the wood and timber thereof to some better use.' At this point, Burbage's sons Cuthbert and Richard took action.

### First glimpse of the Globe?

In 1599, Thomas Platter of Basle recorded: 'After dinner, at about two o'clock, I went with my party across the water; in the straw-thatched house we saw the tragedy of the first Emperor Julius Casear, very pleasantly performed, with approximately fifteen characters; at the end of the play they danced together admirably and exceedingly gracefully, according to their custom, two in each group dressed in men's and two in women's **apparel**.' This could have been the first recorded performance at the newly-erected Globe. It was usual for boy or men actors to dress in women's clothing – there were few actresses, even for romantic roles like Juliet.

On the night of 28 December, with Allen away in the country, they arranged for a group of workmen to dismantle the playhouse, then ferry it across the Thames to Bankside. These materials provided the basis for a new theatre, finer than any seen in London before. Called the Globe, it could hold an audience of 2500 people – and even three years later Allen was trying in vain to sue the company for 'deceiving' him on that winter night.

The recycled Globe, which took six months to build, was a big success. At least 29 plays were written for the company during its first decade there, 16 of them by Shakespeare. Disaster struck in 1613 when the theatre caught fire during a performance and burned to the ground (see page 46–7). Rebuilt, it continued to operate until 1644 when the **Puritan** point of view finally triumphed – abolishing all drama and demolishing England's playhouses.

In the last decade of the 20th century, near to its former site, a new Globe theatre was built in the Shakespearean style on London's South Bank. But little is known for sure about the original theatre. Was it round or many-sided? Was the stage in sunlight or shadow? Did some spectators sit on the stage itself? We cannot be certain.

# King's Man

On 24 March 1603, an era came to an end for the English people. After a reign that stretched back to 1558, Queen Elizabeth I was dead.

Never having married, she had no direct heir to succeed her on the throne. Amid some uncertainty, the succession passed to a **Stuart**, the 37-year-old King James VI of Scotland, who became James I of England. His great-grandmother had been the sister of Elizabeth's father, King Henry VIII.

The public theatres closed, first in mourning for the dead queen, then as a new wave of plague hit London. James made his way south in leisurely fashion, arriving in his new capital in early May. He was a confident, experienced monarch with a quirky independent mind. Many of his English subjects, leading figures in politics and the arts, were not sure that the royal favour and **patronage** they had enjoyed under Elizabeth would be continued. Shakespeare and the Lord Chamberlain's Men were, however, quite safe. On 17 May, James I of England ordered that the company be adopted as his own.

James I, shown here, was King of England from 1603 until 1625. Although intelligent and idealistic, he could also be coarse and vulgar, and had many arguments with his parliaments. Nicknamed 'the wisest fool in **Christendom**', he had a very different personality from the more formal and **regal** Elizabeth I.

James watched the King's Men, as they were now called, on many occasions. The company performed approximately 187 times before him between 1603 and 1616 – even though plays were now being rivalled for popularity by 'masques'. These were lavish entertainments featuring music, dance and words, often based on mythic themes, elaborately staged by such leading architects and designers as Inigo Jones (1573–1652). We have no record of Shakespeare, unlike Ben Jonson, writing masques. But after about 1605, many of his plays included scenes of formal dancing and song, sometimes involving mythical characters. As ever, he was able to detect the mood of the theatre-going public and was prepared to produce work that suited it.

This page from the 1604/5 'Revels Accounts' shows court performances of plays by Shakespeare – or 'Shaxberd' as he is called here. The Master of the Revels listed eleven performances by the King's Men in the year, seven featuring plays written by Shakespeare himself.

> "
> 'Know ye that we… have licensed and authorised… these our servants Lawrence Fletcher, William Shakespeare, Richard Burbage, Augustine Philips, John Heminges, Henry Condell, William Sly, Robert Armin, Richard Cowley and the rest of their associates freely to use and exercise the art and faculty of playing comedies, tragedies, histories, interludes, morals, **pastorals**, stage-plays and such others like… as well for the recreation of our loving subjects, as for our solace and pleasure when we shall think good to see them…'
> "

So reads part of James I's declaration by which the company of the Lord Chamberlain's Men became the King's Men.

## 'A Tale Told by an Idiot'

'Life's but a walking shadow, a poor player
That struts and frets his hour upon the stage,
And then is heard no more. It is a tale
Told by an idiot, full of sound and fury,
Signifying nothing.'

Those lines were spoken by the murderous king Macbeth, in the tragedy that bears his name – one of several tragedies written around 1606. At roughly the same time Shakespeare was writing these rather more optimistic lines at the end of the romance *All's Well That Ends Well*:

'Let us from point to
    point this story know,
To make the even truth
    in pleasure flow...
All yet seems well; and
    if it end so meet,
The bitter past, more
    welcome is the sweet.'

Thanks to his great versatility and **virtuosity**, Shakespeare's tone could shift from 'dark' to 'light' within two scenes of a single play. Yet some scholars note a mainly sombre mood in much of his work in the first decade of the 1600s. From *Hamlet* and *Othello* to *Timon of Athens*, *King Lear* and *Coriolanus*, his tragic heroes were all destined for disaster.

Raphael Holinshed's popular *Chronicles of England, Scotlande and Irelande* (first published in 1577) was a vital source-book for Shakespeare. It gave him information on real historical figures like Richard III and Henry V as well as mythical British monarchs like King Lear. People were more interested in what 'Britain' meant after 1603, since a single king ruled both England and Scotland. By looking to the past, people could forge a new sense of national identity.

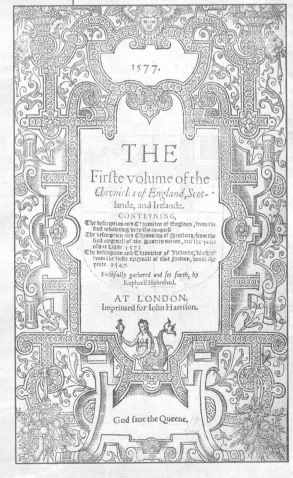

1577.

THE
Firſte volume of the
*Chronicles of England, Scot-*
lande, and Irelande.
CONTEYNING,
The deſcription and Chronicles of England, from the
firſt inhabiting vnto the conqueſt
The deſcription and Chronicles of Scotland, from the
firſt originall of the Scottes nation, till the yeare
of our Lorde 1571
The deſcription and Chronicles of Yrelande, likewiſe
from the firſte originall of that ſtation, vntill the
yeare. 1547.

*Faithfully gathered and ſet forth, by*
Raphaell Holinſhed.

AT LONDON,
Imprinted for Iohn Harriſon.

God ſaue the Queene.

The tragedy *King Lear* was a harrowing play about an ancient British monarch (shown here on the right in a 19th-century painting by Daniel Maclise) who lost all by dividing his kingdom and trying to abdicate his responsibilities. But like the greatest Greek **tragedies**, it is not just frightening and sad but it also finally suggests that good can come from turmoil. Two early printed versions of the play exist, one from 1608, the other from 1623. The differences between the texts probably resulted from changes made during actual performances.

Often there seems to be a dramatic conflict between these characters and forces far beyond their control. 'As flies to wanton boys,' says the Earl of Gloucester in *King Lear*, 'are we to the gods.' At times it seems that peace can be found only in accepting this powerlessness. As Hamlet remarks, 'There's a special providence in the fall of a sparrow. If it be now, 'tis not to come.' Yet plays like *Antony and Cleopatra*, *Hamlet* and *Macbeth* also focus on the need for individual responsibility. All the plays show what can go wrong inside a kingdom or empire if its rulers are not dutiful people of the highest calibre – maybe because Shakespeare was writing in increasingly unsettled times. The **Catholic** Gunpowder Plot to blow up king and parliament was discovered in 1605. And well before mid-century, political and religious tensions would finally lead to civil warfare in many parts of Europe, including England.

## 'Kings hereafter'

*Macbeth* explores the issues of destiny and personal choice in a topical Scottish setting. Three witches meet two generals in the King of Scotland's army. To one, Macbeth, they predict that he will rise to become king. To the other, Banquo, they predict that his heirs will rule Scotland as 'kings hereafter'.

The three witches in Shakespeare's tragedy as painted by Henry Fuseli (1741–1825).

This meeting sets Macbeth and his ruthless wife on a bloodstained, guilt-stricken course that results in them seizing the crown by assassination then losing their own lives. Does 'blind' Fate drive them on? Or are the ambitious pair always responsible for their own actions? Each member of the audience can decide. The play must have struck a chord for James I. He lived in terror of assassination and witchcraft. He also claimed descent from Fleance, the son of the historical Banquo.

## Another venue

As well as his great tragedies, Shakespeare continued to write new plays (usually based on existing stories) that are now called his 'mature' comedies. Plays like *Measure for Measure* had a sharper, sometimes darker edge than his earlier 'light' comedies. Like *All's Well That Ends Well*, it left the audience wondering what the future held for its main characters – Shakespeare no longer seemed so interested in traditional 'happy ever after' endings.

In a number of his later plays, special effects played a key part. Although open air theatres did not provide background scenery, there was always a place for some effects. Cannonballs might have been rolled around to simulate the sound of thunder. Under their costumes, actors hid bladders full of pigs' blood that spurted open when they were stabbed. The King's Men performed indoors too, at court or on tour, but only after 1608 did they put on shows at a permanent indoor theatre, Blackfriars, in fashionable central London.

Measuring only 46 feet by 66 (13.8 metres by 19.8 metres), this was a far more intimate auditorium than the Globe. Only 700 spectators could be admitted, and all of them sat – mostly in front of the stage, but some in boxes or on the stage balcony. The stage itself was lit by candles expensively suspended in great branches, which gave the opportunity for more visual effects than in the open air. Seat prices at the Blackfriars theatre were six times higher than at the Globe, so only the more affluent kind of play-goers attended. Shakespeare's company continued to perform for the whole range of London society at the Globe too – for tradesmen and apprentices as well as for courtiers. In the future, however, it would become more usual for plays to be watched by smaller, 'select' audiences. Shakespeare himself clearly liked the location of the Blackfriars venue. In 1613, he bought his last London property just a couple of hundred metres away.

# SHAKE-SPEARES

## SONNETS.

Neuer before Imprinted.

AT LONDON
By *G. Eld* for *T. T.* and are
to be folde by *Iohn Wright*, dwelling
at Chrift Church gate.
1 6 0 9.

TO.THE.ONLIE.BEGETTER.OF.
THESE.INSVING.SONNETS.
Mr. W. H. ALL.HAPPINESSE.
AND.THAT.ETERNITIE.
PROMISED.

BY.

OVR.EVER-LIVING.POET.

WISHETH.

THE.WELL-WISHING.
ADVENTVRER.IN.
SETTING.
FORTH.

T. T.

Here we see the title and dedication pages of Shakespeare's *Sonnets*, from 1609. This whole project is shrouded in mystery – we cannot even be sure of the identity of the 'Mr W.H.' to whom the 154 poems are dedicated. Unlike the title pages of Shakespeare's earlier published poetry (see page 22), this one openly proclaims the famous author's name.

## Shakespeare's 'spiritual biography'?

In 1609, the year after his mother's death, Shakespeare published a new volume of verse. It consists of 154 **sonnets**, short poems of fourteen lines, possibly written over a long period of time, based on themes of love and betrayal. They express so many shades of passion with such skill and verve that the collection has been called the poet's own 'spiritual biography'. Typically with the ever-elusive Shakespeare, however, it yields little factual detail about him.

The sequence of poems seems to trace a relationship between three people: a poet, a young man and a 'woman coloured ill', who is often called 'the dark lady'. We cannot even be sure if the poet is Shakespeare, let alone who the other two people might be – although for many years that has not stopped scholars and experts from speculating. Some of them now see the sequence as 'a fictional exploration of despair and loss'. If so, the intense emotional pain it displays can only confirm Shakespeare as a creative genius of the first rank.

> "                                                                    "
> 'O! how much more doth beauty beauteous seem
> By that sweet ornament which truth doth give:
> The rose looks fair, but fairer we it deem
> For that sweet odour which doth in it live.
> The canker-blooms have full as deep a dye
> As the perfumed tincture of the roses,
> Hang on such thorns, and play as wantonly
> When summer's breath their masked buds discloses:
> But, for their virtue only is their show,
> They live unwoo'd and unrespected fade;
> Die to themselves. Sweet roses do not so;
> Of their sweet deaths are sweetest odours made:
>     And so of you, beauteous and lovely youth,
>     When that shall fade, by verse distils your truth.'
> Sonnet 54

# The years of looking back

We cannot be sure when Shakespeare's playwriting career in London began. Nor do we know precisely when it ended. We do not even know if all his 'late plays' were written by him alone, or in partnership with collaborators. But if these late plays had a common theme, it was a tendency to look back to the past. Maybe this was inevitable, since the playwright was approaching his own life's end.

*Pericles*, a romance about a prince of Tyre, looked back to the work of the 14th-century poet John Gower. (Although immensely popular with audiences in the early 1600s, this play was left out of the First Folio of 1623 since another man, George Wilkins, partly wrote it.) *The Two Noble Kinsmen*, co-authored with John Fletcher, looked back to another great medieval poet, Geoffrey Chaucer, who wrote *The Canterbury Tales*. In *The Winter's Tale*, Shakespeare based his plot on a story by a man who had figured in his own early career. This was Robert Greene, the rival playwright who in 1592 attacked him as an 'upstart Crow' and '*Johannes Factotum*' (see page 16).

Meanwhile in *Cymbeline* Shakespeare returned to Holinshed's *Chronicle* (see page 39) for information on a story set in ancient, pre-Christian Britain. With John Fletcher, he even looked back to more recent English history in *Henry VIII*, set during the reign of Queen Elizabeth I's father. But his most original work of **retrospection** was *The Tempest*, one of Shakespeare's shortest plays and one of his most memorably moving.

## 'My project... was to please'

Set on a lonely island, *The Tempest* is dominated by the ageing magician Prospero, a shipwrecked former Duke of Milan. Shakespeare included special effects that could be staged at the indoor Blackfriars theatre – like making a whole banquet 'disappear' with the help of pulleys and trapdoors. Prospero uses his magical powers to gain revenge on the men who have seized his dukedom years before, and also to find a husband for his daughter Miranda. The play is full of beautiful, often-quoted passages. 'O brave new world,' cries Miranda when she sets eyes on the first men she has ever seen apart from her father, 'That has such people in't.' At the end of the action Prospero, upon giving up his magic, addresses the audience in this way in a frank appeal for applause:

'Now my charms are all o'erthrown,
And what strength I have's mine own;
Which is most faint: now, 'tis true,
I must be here confined by you,
Or sent to Naples…
But release me from my bands,
With the help of your good hands.
Gentle breath of yours my sails
Must fill, or else my project fails,
Which was to please.'

Although Shakespeare lived for five more years after writing this play, many scholars believe he saw Prospero as a fictional version of himself. As a magician with words, maybe he was preparing for the day when he too would have to set aside his great powers. The play was one of several performed by the King's Men at court in 1613 to celebrate the wedding of James I's daughter Elizabeth to the German Prince Frederick of the Palatinate. Its shortness must have appealed to the king, who notoriously disliked long entertainments.

This character, Caliban, comes from a modern production of Shakespeare's The Tempest.

This book, published in 1598, shows the 'ghost' of the writer Robert Greene still at work. Shakespeare helped to 're-animate' him by closely basing his play *The Winter's Tale* on Greene's *Pandosto*. The play is a tragi-comedy in which Leontes suspects his wife has been unfaithful, and so his children are not really his own. By the play's end his suspicions are lifted and everyone's true identity is confirmed.

GREENE IN CONCEIPT.

New raifed from his graue to write the Tragique Hiftorie of faire *Valeria* of London.

WHEREIN IS TRVLY DISCOVERED the rare and lamentable iffue of a Hu, bands dotage, a wiues lewdneffe, & childrens difobedience.

*Receiued and reported by I. D.*

*Veritas non quærit angulos, vmbra gaudet.*

Printed at London by R ICHARD BRADOCKE for *William Iones,* dwelling at the figne of the Gunne neare Holborne conduit. 1598.

## The Globe dissolves

On the afternoon of 29 June 1613, the Globe theatre's audience was treated to a lavishly spectacular play about King Henry VIII, full of effects and illusions. It was written by Shakespeare, possibly in collaboration with John Fletcher (see picture). The play was originally entitled *All is True*. This implied that all the ceremonial events shown on stage really took place at King Henry's court – and maybe that all the rest was historically accurate too. (In the First Folio of 1623, its name was changed to the more historical-sounding *Henry VIII*.)

For one effect, gunners had to fire some small cannons up towards the thatched roof. Henry Wootton, a **diplomat**, happened to be in the theatre on the fateful afternoon. He described what happened: 'King Henry making a masque at the Cardinal Wolsey's house, and certain chambers being shot off at his entry, some of the paper, or other stuff, wherewith one of them was stuffed, did light on the thatch, where being thought at first but an idle smoke, and their eyes more attentive to the show, it kindled inwardly, and ran round like a train, consuming within less than an hour the whole house to the very grounds.'

Rising young playwright John Fletcher may have co-written two of Shakespeare's later plays. Literary collaboration of this kind was quite common throughout the period. Fletcher – the son of the Bishop of London and probably educated at Cambridge – eventually succeeded Shakespeare as the King's Men's 'ordinary' or resident playwright.

Amazingly, although nothing was left of the theatre after the blaze, there seems to have been just one minor casualty. 'One man had his breeches set on fire,' wrote Wootton, 'that would perhaps have broiled him, if he had not by the benefit of a provident **wit** put it out with bottle ale.' Within a year, a new Globe had been built, this time with a tiled roof.

But Shakespeare did not contribute, and at that point he probably sold his own share in the company. Some **Puritans** believed that 'the sudden fearful burning' was a deliberate act of God – that He had set the Globe on fire to show His displeasure at the sinful world of the theatre. Ironically in *The Tempest*, Shakespeare's Prospero had already foreseen:

'The cloud-capped towers, the gorgeous palaces,
The solemn temples, the great globe itself,
Yea, all which it inherit, shall dissolve…'

# 'Sweet Swan of Avon'

Shakespeare may not have written his very last theatrical masterpieces in London. From 1610, he spent more and more of his time in Stratford. He had bought more property in the town, including 107 acres of land at Welcombe on Stratford's northern boundary. Presumably he wanted to enjoy Stratford, as well as creating *Cymbeline*, *The Winter's Tale* and *The Tempest*.

But he still made trips to London, maybe now just to help to put on plays rather than act in them, and he probably never even thought about retirement. Few people in **Tudor** or **Stuart** times lived long enough to consider it. Old people were most admired when they kept at their work until close to death. In Shakespeare's own plays, King Lear suffers terribly after seeking leisure at the end of his life; and the aged Prospero in *The Tempest* returns to Milan to be Duke again. The top of the monument to Shakespeare in Stratford church (see picture) shows two naked boys, one representing 'Labour', the other 'Rest'. The hand of the latter holds a skull, to show that only in death can a man find true rest.

SHAKESPEARE'S MONUMENT.

This monument to Shakespeare stands in Holy Trinity Church, Stratford. It was made by the Southwark sculptor Gerard Johnson. Surviving members of Shakespeare's family **commissioned** it, so they must have been satisfied that it looked like him. One modern scholar, however, likened the expression to that of 'a self-satisfied pork butcher'!

## Preparing for death

In Shakespeare's time, men usually made wills when they felt they did not have long to live. This may have been Shakespeare's reason for making one in January 1616. A re-written version of this will has survived – including a rare example of the playwright's signature – and it gives us a fascinating, and slightly mystifying, snapshot of his life just before he died.

Shakespeare had one sad reason for re-writing his will. At the time of the original version, his younger daughter Judith was about to marry a Stratford wine merchant called Thomas Quiney. Shakespeare's will includes a **dowry** payment of £100. The marriage went ahead, with Judith already pregnant. But then another woman claimed to be having a child of Quiney's too, out of wedlock. She and the baby died in childbirth in March, and Thomas was punished in the church courts. In his re-written will, Shakespeare excluded the **promiscuous** Quiney. Only Judith was now to inherit the £100, and some other small items.

His elder daughter, the wife of Dr John Hall (see page 51), fared much better. Shakespeare left New Place to her and her highly respectable husband, plus the other properties and most of the contents of those houses. Other **bequests** included £10 for the poor of Stratford – which a man of his wealth could quite easily afford – and some small sums for three of his colleagues in the King's Men: Richard Burbage, John Heminges and Henry Condell. This money was to pay for rings that they could wear in memory of him after his death – a common practice at the time.

As for his wife Anne, Shakespeare mentioned her only towards the end of the document – and even then, not by name. 'I give unto my wife my second-best bed,' he dictated, adding that she could also have its 'furniture' or bed linen. This might seem ungenerous in their 34th year of marriage. Maybe it was just a token of love and affection (a home's best bed would have been reserved for special guests, so the second-best may have been the married couple's own). As his widow, Anne would also have received a share of her husband's goods and property. But this single mention in the will could suggest a coolness

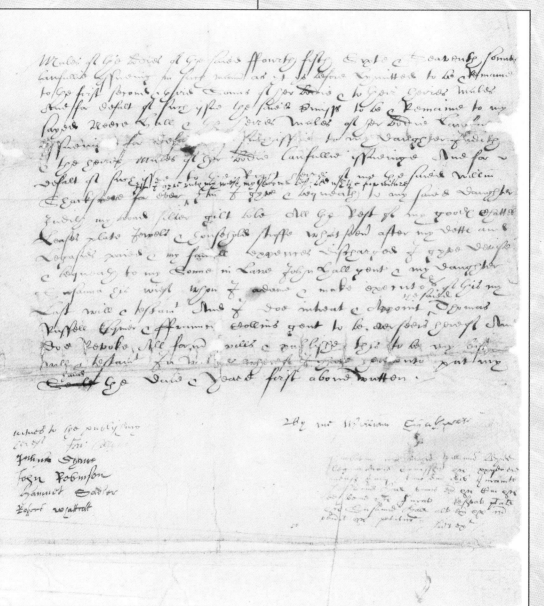

between husband and wife. Anne outlived Shakespeare by seven years, and died in 1623 at the age of 67. Her bones were then laid to the left of the playwright's gravestone, on which was inscribed the verse reproduced on page 5. Maybe Shakespeare himself made it up. It was meant to stop anyone from moving his remains to the charnel house – the place where dead bodies or bones were stored – as sometimes happened.

## 'My life is run his compass'

In Shakespeare's play *Julius Caesar*, the character Cassius says just before he dies on his own birthday: 'This day I breathed first; time is come round,/And where I did begin, there shall I end;/My life is run his compass.' It is quite possible that Shakespeare too died on the same day of the year as his birthday. 23 April 1616 could well have been his 52nd birthday, and that was when his life 'ran his compass'. In the same parish register that recorded his baptism we can read that 'Will Shakspere, gent.' was buried in Holy Trinity Church two days later.

What caused Shakespeare's death? On that, the records are silent. During any last illness he was probably treated by his son-in-law Dr John Hall, and he had the rest of his family around him. Within the next 50 years, a story went around that Shakespeare died in an unfortunate way. John Ward, a Stratford doctor and clergyman, recorded a local tradition that 'Shakespeare, [Michael] Drayton and Ben Jonson had a merry meeting, and it seems drank too hard, for Shakespeare died of a fever there contracted.'

There is no way of confirming this. If Jonson did visit his old friend and rival, he may well have told him about his ambitious scheme to collect up all his own stage works and publish them in a huge volume. The task of producing a similar volume for Shakespeare, the First Folio, would be left to two of the men who would wear memorial rings for him – Heminges and Condell (see page 49). And Jonson would help to adorn that work in a poetic tribute to the man he called 'Sweet Swan of Avon':

'Thou art a Monument, without a tomb,
And art alive still, while thy Booke doth live,
And we have wits to read, and praise to give...'

# The man and his work

In 1604, a young gentleman named Antony Scoloker published a book entitled *Diaphantus*. In it he discussed what a good piece of writing should ideally be like. His first example was *Arcadia* by Sir Philip Sidney 'where the Prose and Verse, (Matter and Words) are like his Mistress's eyes, one still excelling another.' Then he continued, 'Or to come home to the vulgar's element, like friendly Shakespeare's tragedies, where the comedian rides when the tragedian stands on tip-toe: faith, it should please all, like Prince *Hamlet*.'

'Vulgar' here means popular – Shakespeare's plays could be enjoyed by everyone, including the uneducated. Many people today think of *Hamlet* as a **highbrow** work of art. Scoloker made it clear that around 1600 the play could 'please all.' (We can even trace how popular it was, from the number of boys who were given the name 'Hamlet' in the early 1600s.) *King Lear* and *Macbeth* also caught the public imagination as deep **tragedies** that still had plenty of mad

Actors playing Hamlet have been lifting skulls and uttering the famous line, 'Alas poor Yorick!' for over four hundred years.

### Shakespeare's most famous speech?

'To be, or not to be; that is the question;
Whether 'tis nobler in the mind to suffer
The slings and arrows of outrageous fortune,
Or to take arms against a sea of troubles,
And, by opposing, end them…
Thus conscience doth make cowards of us all,
And thus the native hue of resolution
Is sicklied o'er by the pale cast of thought
And enterprises of great pith and moment
With this regard their currents turn awry,
And lose the name of action.'

This extract comes from *Hamlet*, a magnificent tragedy of revenge. Hamlet, maybe Shakespeare's best-known character, has struck a chord with generation after generation.

scenes and comic moments. Likewise **comedies** like *Measure for Measure* and *All's Well That Ends Well* could almost be seen as tragedies. A single Shakespearean play could touch so many bases for so many different kinds of theatre-goer. And for almost four centuries since his death, the magic has continued to work, not just in the English language but also in translation.

## England's true patron?

We know very little about Shakespeare's life and personality, yet he is famous the world over. His unparalleled body of work as a playwright and poet has established his reputation for all time. But although Shakespeare the man remains elusive, he continues to inspire affection as well as admiration.

Maybe because he is so elusive, each entranced reader or theatregoer is able to imagine him, and relate to him, in his or her own way. In that sense, he has become less like a historical person than a well-loved semi-mythical figure such as Robin Hood or King Arthur. A third figure of this kind is St George, England's patron saint, whose festival day on 23 April is now celebrated as much for Shakespeare's birth and death as it is for the old Christian dragon-slayer.

# The influence of Shakespeare

In *Hamlet*, a **troupe** of actors puts on a play within the main play. Before they perform, the Prince of Denmark addresses them – maybe in a way that Shakespeare the director once addressed the King's Men before a production:

'... the purpose of playing... was and is, to hold, as 'twere, the mirror up to nature; to show virtue her own feature, scorn her own image, and the very age and body of the time his form and pressure.'

Hamlet was saying that plays can show people as they really are, not as they might like to see themselves, and that they can reflect the world outside too. This has always been an aim of truly great art, and few would deny that Shakespeare achieved it repeatedly, not just for his own time but for ours as well – for new performances of his plays are staged every year all over the world. His creative influence extends further still. Just as Shakespeare himself drew heavily on the work of others, countless later poets, playwrights, authors, painters, composers and film-makers have used his work as an inspiration – putting their own spin on his plots and characters.

## Shakespeare and music

In Shakespeare's time, only a few trumpet blasts might accompany the action on stage. Later composers – from the German Brahms and the Austrian Schubert to the Russian Tchaikovsky, the American Bernstein and the Italian Verdi – wrote marvellous music for songs, symphonic poems, musicals, ballets and operas inspired by Shakespeare's theatrical works. Possibly the most famous piece composed for a Shakespeare performance was written by Felix Mendelssohn (1809–47). Part of his incidental music for *A Midsummer Night's Dream* is still played today as 'The Wedding March'. Even the 1996 film *William Shakespeare's Romeo & Juliet* has a soundtrack featuring songs by bands like Radiohead, The Cardigans and Garbage, which became a best-selling album.

## A mirror still held up to nature

'Read him, therefore,' wrote Heminges and Condell in their introductory words to Shakespeare's First Folio of 1623, 'and again, and again.' Their advice has not fallen on deaf ears. From 1624, a copy of the First Folio was kept in Oxford University's Bodleian Library. During the reign of King Charles I (1625–49), some parts of its pages were entirely worn away by the friction of eager students' fingers and resting elbows. These early readers seemed to dwell longest over Shakespeare's love poetry and on the play *Romeo and Juliet* – particularly the 'balcony scene' between the two young lovers.

Ophelia, a tragic character in Shakespeare's *Hamlet*, has inspired several painters. This painting of her is by John William Waterhouse (1847–1917).

Since then, Shakespeare's works have never really gone out of fashion. Today, nearly four hundred years later, *Romeo and Juliet* is the play of his that teachers most often encourage their pupils to read first (followed by *Julius Caesar* and *Macbeth*). The 'uneducated' poet and playwright from Stratford-upon-Avon thus continues to influence the way that each new generation sees itself. For although he did not travel the world himself, the proud English gentleman William Shakespeare created a complete world of his own – one that still comes to life every time an enduring line of his is read or spoken.

Shakespeare's work has overcome many cultural barriers. Here the Japanese director Yukio Ninagawa presents his own take on *Macbeth*.

# Timeline

| | |
|---|---|
| **c.1557** | Shakespeare's father John marries Mary Arden |
| **1558** | Elizabeth I becomes Queen of England |
| **1564** | William Shakespeare born in Stratford-upon-Avon; baptized in Holy Trinity Church |
| **1567** | Public playhouse the Red Lion opens in London |
| **1568–9** | John Shakespeare serves as **Bailiff** of Stratford |
| **1572** | Leicester's Men perform at Stratford |
| **1574** | Warwick's Men perform at Stratford |
| **1575** | Festivities at Kenilworth Castle to mark visit of Queen Elizabeth I |
| **1576** | James Burbage builds the Theatre in London |
| **1577** | Raphael Holinshed's *Chronicles* first published |
| **1580** | One of the last performances of the great cycle of **mystery plays** acted by the craft guilds at Coventry – maybe witnessed by Shakespeare who lives nearby |
| **1582** | Shakespeare marries Anne Hathaway |
| **1583** | Birth of Shakespeare's daughter Susanna; formation of new company of players, the Queen's Men |
| **1585** | Birth of Shakespeare's twins Hamnet and Judith |
| **1587** | Expulsion of John Shakespeare from Corporation of Stratford; possible date for Shakespeare's move from Stratford to London; execution of Mary Queen of Scots, mother of future James I of England |
| **1588** | Failed attempt by Spanish Armada to land in England |
| **1592** | Personal attack on Shakespeare in Robert Greene's *Groatsworth of Wit* |
| **1592–3** | Plague closes London theatres |
| **1593** | Publication of Shakespeare's poem *Venus and Adonis* |
| **1594** | Publication of Shakespeare's poem *The Rape of Lucrece*; Shakespeare's *The Comedy of Errors* performed at Gray's Inn |

**1595** Shakespeare a member of Lord Chamberlain's Men who perform at court

**1596** Death of Shakespeare's son Hamnet; Shakespeare applies (successfully) to College of Arms for his father to be made a gentleman

**1597** Shakespeare buys New Place, the second-largest house in Stratford; Shakespeare listed as a tax-defaulter in London

**1598** Shakespeare listed for hoarding corn and malt in Stratford

**1599** Globe theatre built in Southwark; Swiss traveller Thomas Platter records watching Shakespeare's *Julius Caesar* in London

**1601** Shakespeare's *Richard II* performed at the Globe by Lord Chamberlain's Men; Earl of Essex attempts **coup** in London and is executed, while Shakespeare's patron the Earl of Southampton is put in the Tower of London; poem by Shakespeare, *The Phoenix and the Turtle*, is published; John Shakespeare dies

**1602** Shakespeare's *Twelfth Night* is performed at the **Middle Temple**

**1603** Queen Elizabeth I dies and is succeeded by King James I; Lord Chamberlain's Men now become King's Men

**1603–4** Shakespeare plays major role at court in Ben Jonson's tragedy *Sejanus his Fall*

**1604** Five or more plays by Shakespeare performed at court in November and December

**1605** Shakespeare buys portion of **tithes** in and near Stratford; Gunpowder Plotters are foiled attempting to blow up the King and parliament

**1607** Marriage of Susanna Shakespeare to John Hall in Stratford; burial of Shakespeare's brother Edmund, an actor, in Southwark, London

**1608** Birth of Shakespeare's grand-daughter Elizabeth Hall; death of Shakespeare's mother Mary; publication of *The History of King Lear*

| | | | |

| | |
|---|---|
| **1608–9** | King's Men begin to perform at indoor Blackfriars theatre |
| **1609** | Severe wave of plague closes London theatres; publication of Shakespeare's **Sonnets** with *A Lover's Complaint* |
| **1610** | Shakespeare's *The Tempest* performed at court |
| **1613** | Marriage of king's daughter Elizabeth to Frederick, Elector Palatine; Shakespeare buys property at Blackfriars, London; Globe theatre burns to ground and is rebuilt within a year; fire in Stratford destroys 54 houses, none owned by Shakespeare |
| **1614** | Opening of rebuilt Globe theatre, probably now without Shakespeare as a sharer |
| **1616** | Shakespeare dictates two drafts of his will, either side of marriage of his daughter Judith to Stratford tradesman Thomas Quiney; Shakespeare dies and is buried in Holy Trinity Church, Stratford |
| **1619** | Death of Richard Burbage, leading King's Man and former colleague of Shakespeare |
| **1623** | Death of Shakespeare's widow Anne; publication of *Mr William Shakespeare's Comedies, Histories & Tragedies* – otherwise known as the First Folio – edited by Shakespeare's friends and fellow King's Men John Heminges and Henry Condell |

# Works by William Shakespeare

There is much dispute about when and in what order Shakespeare wrote his plays. Below are the plays included in the First Folio of 1623. It excluded *Pericles* and *The Two Noble Kinsmen*, which may have been co-written.

## Histories

*King John*
*Richard II*
*Henry IV (Parts 1 and 2)*
*Henry V*
*Henry VI (Parts 1, 2 and 3)*
*Richard III*
*Henry VIII*

## Comedies

*Troilus and Cressida*
*The Tempest*
*The Two Gentlemen of Verona*
*The Merry Wives of Windsor*
*Measure for Measure*
*The Comedy of Errors*
*Much Ado About Nothing*
*Love's Labours Lost*
*A Midsummer Night's Dream*
*The Merchant of Venice*
*As You Like It*
*The Taming of the Shrew*
*All's Well That Ends Well*
*Twelfth Night*
*The Winter's Tale*

## Tragedies

*Coriolanus*
*Titus Andronicus*
*Romeo and Juliet*
*Timon of Athens*
*Julius Caesar*
*Macbeth*
*Hamlet*
*King Lear*
*Othello*
*Antony and Cleopatra*
*Cymbeline*

They can be found, along with the poetry, in *William Shakespeare: The Complete Works*, edited by Gary Taylor and Stanley Wells (Oxford University Press, 1986). Editions of individual plays are available in the *New Penguin Shakespeare* series.

# Glossary

**alms**  charitable donations to the poor

**apparel**  clothing

**bachelors**  unmarried men

**Bailiff**  high-ranking local official

**benefactor**  person who gives friendly, practical help

**bequest**  money or goods passed on from one person to another

**burgess**  influential town official

**Catholic**  religion of most of the Christians in western Europe before, in some countries, the Protestants split away to set up their own churches in the 16th century.

**chiding**  telling off

**Christendom**  all lands where people followed the Christian religion

**coat of arms**  well-to-do person's distinguishing badge

**coin**  to make up or invent

**comedies**  plays of a mainly light and amusing nature, often dealing with everyday matters, and usually having a happy ending

**commission**  arranging with a creative artist that a piece of work should be produced and paid for

**conspicuous**  highly visible, obvious

**contagion**  communication of disease from person to person

**contemporaries**  people who live at the same time as you

**coup**  overthrow of the government

**critics**  professional writers who study an author's life and work

**curer**  person who treats animal skins to make them usable

**demise**  death

**dens of iniquity**  slang term for places where bad behaviour occurs

**diplomat**  person who negotiates with a foreign government on behalf of his own government

**divers**  different, varying, old spelling of diverse

**dowry** amount of money or property that a wife takes to her husband on marriage

**dynasty** family that for a period rules a country

**economic recession** economic issues involve the production and distribution of wealth; in periodic times of recession, there is quite clearly not enough wealth to go round

**editions** versions; all the copies of a work published at one time

**enmity** hatred between people

**epistle** letter, introductory verse in the form of a letter

**fawning** flattering, in a creepy way

**forbear** avoid doing something

**frontispiece** illustration opposite the title page of a book

**highbrow** culturally superior, highly intellectual

**languish** suffer

**Latins** in this sense, ancient Romans (Latin was their language)

**mercer** dealer in textile fabrics

**Middle Temple** one of the 'inns of court' in London (both the building and the society that used it), to which lawyers belonged

**mystery plays** plays performed by groups of craftsmen at the Christian festival of Corpus Christi

**odious** hateful

**Orient** old-fashioned word for the East, including China and India

**parish** area of the country with its own church and local church official

**pastoral** to do with country life

**patent** certificate proving your right to something

**patron** rich person who supports the arts

**patronage** support or encouragement given by a rich person – called a patron – to a creative one

**promiscuous** sexually unfaithful

**propaganda** information that supports or advertises a particular point of view or set of beliefs

**Protestant** Christians who rejected the teachings of the Catholic church that was headed by the Pope in Rome. England remained a Protestant country from the start of the reign of Elizabeth.

**province** in this context, area of interest or business

**provinces** any part of the country outside the capital, London

**Puritan** deeply committed Protestants who believed that Christians should behave in a pure and decent way at all times

**quarter** measure from pre-decimal times (equals one quarter of a 'hundredweight')

**regal** kingly, queenly

**retrospection** looking back

**romanticize** make up romantic stories about someone or something

**sonnet** fourteen line poem with ten syllables per line

**sovereign** supreme ruler of a country

**standing army** professional army; army of men whose only job is to be soldiers

**status** standing or position in society

**Stuart** family name of England's ruling dynasty from 1603 to 1714, originally Scottish, which came after the Tudors

**suitor** man pursuing a woman with marriage in mind

**tithes** in this sense, rights to collect local taxes and keep the profits

**toleration** official acceptance or permission

**tragedies** largely serious plays that show the downfall of a hero and the suffering and death that result from it

**troupe** band, company of actors

**Tudor** family name of England's ruling dynasty from 1485 to 1603

**undergraduates** students working for their degrees

**virtuosity** very high level of talent and ability

**wit** cleverness, understanding

# Places of interest and further reading

## Places to visit and websites

*The Globe, London, SE1, UK* – a reconstruction of the original Globe, includes theatre and exhibition

*The Royal Shakespeare Company, Stratford, UK* – the RSC performs plays in three theatres, the RST, the Swan and the Other Place

*Anne Hathaway's Cottage, Shottery, near Stratford, UK* – the childhood home of Shakespeare's wife

*The Shakespeare Centre, Stratford, UK* – here you can visit Shakespeare's birthplace and the visitor's centre

*www.rsc.org.uk* – Royal Shakespeare Company, details of play performances; education packs

*www.shakespeare.org.uk* – Shakespeare Birthplace Trust, details of local history and Shakespeare properties in Stratford

*www.shakepeares-globe.org/home.htm* – recreation of the Globe theatre on London's South Bank

## Further reading and sources

*The Cambridge Companion to Shakespeare on Film*, ed. Russell Jackson (Cambridge University Press, 2000)

*The Oxford Companion to Shakespeare*, eds Michael Dobson and Stanley Wells (Oxford University Press, 2001)

*Shakespeare*, Germaine Greer (OUP Past Masters series, 1986)

*Shakespeare in the Movies*, Douglas Brode (OUP, 2000)

*Shakespeare: A Life*, Park Honan (Clarendon Press, 1998)

*Shakespeare Man of Theatre*, W. Greenhill and P. Wignall (Reed Educational, 1999)

*Shakespeare: The Poet and his Plays*, Stanley Wells (Methuen, 2001)

*William Shakespeare*, Terry Eagleton (Blackwell, 1986)

*William Shakespeare*, S. Schoenbaum (OUP, 1986)*Ungentle Shakespeare*, K. Duncan-Jones (Arden Shakespeare, 2001)

# Index